The Hell with Taking Notes

Challenging the Status Quo

By Thomas L. Hodge

Table of Contents

-For the moments that you realize

There is a better way to do things...

And it does not match what everyone else believes

Plus it actually works.-

The Effects of Note Taking and Participation

On Classroom Information Processing

How information is encoded into long-term memory and retrieved determines how well the information is remembered. Being able to remember information serves as the fundamental basis of learning new information. The US Department of Education (2008) noted a need for increasing the standards for education. By increasing such standards, students will need to learn more information at a quicker rate than prior generations. To increase learning, students will need to store and retrieve information in a more efficient manner.

How the information is presented to students determines how the information is stored in memory and retrieved from memory.

The style of instruction determines the information is presented to the students. The two most common styles of instruction are lecture-based instruction and participation-based instruction. The lecture method presents information to individuals in a passive manner that facilitates learning by having the individuals take notes on the presentation of information in order to retain information (Marcuse, 1951). In recent decades, interactive participation-based forms of instruction have gained increasing popularity as an effective means of instruction that has challenged the traditional lecture-based approach to teaching (Hardman, Smith, & Wall, 2004). The two approaches utilize differing techniques for having individuals retain the information that is taught. In the lecture method, note taking serves as a primary means of retaining the information. The participation-based model of teaching focuses on interactions between peers and between the student and instructor. This method of immersing the student in the information as an active participant aids in retaining the information that is being taught. In order to explain how these methods account for information learned, research in cognitive psychology examines the underlying mechanisms that encode, organize, and retrieve learned information during classroom instruction.

Structure of Memory

Memory is the mental capacity of an individual to store and recall or recognize facts, events, and impressions. Atkinson and Shiffrin (1968) explained that memory can be divided into the sensory register and short-term and long-term memory systems. The sensory register holds incoming information from the environment for no more than a second. The short-term memory only stores information for 20 to 30 seconds unless attention is given to the information. The widely accepted model proposed that information is selectively transferred from ashort-term memory to long-term memory based on rehearsal of the information. After 20 to 30 seconds, the information is forgotten if it is not attended to or moved into long-term memory. Tulving (1993) divided long-term memory into episodic, semantic, and procedural memory. Episodic memory consists of events that happen to the individual; procedural memory consists of the individual's knowledge of how to perform specific tasks; semantic memory consists of general information about the world.

Baddley (1986) expanded the model of short-term memory by introducing the concept of the working memory. The working memory model served to explain short-term memory by describing it as the functioning component of memory. As opposed to a static and passive entity, working memory is active. It manipulates information by attending to that information. Through attention, working memory can rehearse and elaborate on learned information by making connections between concepts and ideas. These connections improve the storage of such items as they are being encoded into long-term storage. Einstein and McDaniels (2004) explained that encoding is the storing of information into long-term memory. This process is similar to storing information into a filing system. Memory traces are the items being stored in long-term memory (Tulving, 1983). Retrieval is the process of later accessing the memory traces from long term memory for use. The working memory model showed how short-term memory is the functioning part of the memory system that stores and retrieves the memory traces to and from the long-term memory system.

In long-term memory, the organization of memory traces plays a significant role in how easily they are later retrieved by the working memory. When the information is available and a retrieval cue is provided, the working memory is able to retrieve the memory trace from long-term memory for use. As information is stored in a more organized manner, the information is more easily retrieved from long-term memory. A variety of cognitive mechanisms and techniques facilitate the encoding and retrieval of information from long-term memory. Peterson and Peterson (1959) examined rehearsal as a mechanism for remembering information. Rehearsal is the act of repeating items silently to hold the items in memory. They found that the introduction of multiple items decreased the effectiveness of rehearsal on remembering information. In addition to organization, the novelty and uniqueness of the information increases the likelihood of the information being easily retrieved from long-term memory. Tulving and Madigan (1970) described elaboration coding, which is also called elaboration, as the process of providing more detail to information and making more connections between concepts to improve the storage and retrieval of such information. The elaboration of information creates unique connections between previously known information and the newly learned information.

Semantic Memory

In classroom environments, the type of information being taught to students is mostly semantic information. Semantic information, which is stored in semantic memory, includes facts, dates, rules, and various concepts about the world that an individual learns. Semantic memories are organized and stored in long-term memory through several organizational methods. Anderson, Reynolds, Schallert, and Goetz (1977) proposed that semantic information is divided into schemata, broad generalizable features of items, and stored in long-term memory as the components of the original item with multiple connections between the components. As the number and strength of the connections is greater, the information is more easily retrieved from long-term memory. Smith, Shoben, and Rips (1974) proposed that the schemata could be categorized into features that are characteristic and features that are defining of the memory. The defining features present information as being novel and standing out from characteristic features. The characteristic features are typical of the generalized category to which the new information belongs.

Collins and Loftus (1975) proposed the Collins and Loftus Network Model, which organized memories into a network of interconnected concepts and items. When an individual accesses one item, other items associated with the accessed item are also activated and indirectly accessed. As one develops more connections to an item, it is easier for the particular item to be accessed by the short-term memory. In addition to explaining the recall of verbal items in a laboratory setting, McNamara and Holbrook (2003) demonstrated that the Collins and Loftus Network Model could also be used to explain the priming effects that are essential in the recall of semantic information. The Collins and Loftus Network Model demonstrated how information is more easily recalled by make more connections to the information that is to be recalled.

Depth of Processing Approach

Building on the Collins and Loftus Network Model (Collins & Loftus, 1972), the depth of processing approach to memory concludes that as information is more strongly associated with existing memories and other related concepts, a memory will become more easily retrieved from long-term memory. Craik and Lockhart (1972) explained that information is stored in long-term memory in a manner that is more easily accessed when the information is more meaningful than when information is shallow and without meaning. The depth of processing approach focuses on the distinctiveness of the information. The distinctiveness allows the working memory to differentiate the information from similar concepts. The depth of processing approach also focuses on the elaboration of the information to create connections between the new information and other concepts to allow quicker access to the information.

Craik and Lockhart (1972) compared how individuals retained structural information, phonetic information, and semantic information. They found that individuals better retained phonetic information, the way a word sounds, than structural information, the way a word looks. Semantic information, the meaning of the word, was more easily retrieved than both structural and phonetic information. The different types of information were viewed as having varying qualities of depth in how they were processed. The information that was more easily retrieved from memory had formed more connections with associated schemata and concepts. These connections gave the information more depth and a quality of being more easily retrieved from long-term memory by the working memory for use. Craik and Lockhart (1972) established three levels of depth to which information can be processed. . Visual processing serves as the first level, phonetic processing serves as the second level, and semantic processing serves as the third level.

Rogers, Kuiper, and Kirker (1977) found that information processed in reference to the individual's self was retained at a deeper level than the semantic information that was not processed in reference to the individual. The self-reference effect adds a fourth level to the depth of processing approach. The self-reference effect can be explained by the large number of connections to and from the individual's concept of self. Self is always present in all autobiographical memories that an individual has in their memory. The self is connected to a greater number of memory traces than other concepts stored in the long-term memory. These connections make the self the strongest item in long-term memory. By having a direct connection to self, the new concept also has secondary connections develop in relation to other concepts that are connected to the concept of the self through this reference. This connection provides a deeper level of processing than general semantic information that is not self-referenced.

Encoding Specificity

Moscovitch and Craik (1976) demonstrated that individuals recalled more information if the conditions during retrieval matched the conditions during encoding. This effect is called the encoding specificity principle. The research demonstrated that matching contexts for encoding and retrieval improved the ability of the individual to recall information even with information that was shallow in nature. This research appeared to contradict the levels of processing approach to learning information. The study utilized rhyming lists of words and recall of the words to demonstrate the encoding specificity principle. The lists produced the effect when the words did not have meaning, but the effect was not significant when the words had meaning. The effect was attributed to the rhyming pattern serving as a stronger and more accurate cue for retrieval than the semantic meaning of the words.

Nairne (2005) found that the encoding specificity principle produced stronger effects in situations that required recall as opposed to recognition. The effects also diminished over longer periods of time more quickly than semantic and self-referenced material, which has strong cognitive connections to other lasting information. A variety of motor, physical, and mental cues led to an improvement in the recall of the previously encoded information in testing situations that are similar to the learning situations (Woodall & Folger, 1981). Information that is processed from a stimulus that is visual will be more easily retrieved as a visual representation that is similar to the encoded stimuli. Verbal information is also better retrieved in the same form in which it was encoded.

Dual Coding Theory

The cognitive model of working memory describes a phonological loop and visuospatial sketchpad as two primary subsystems that manipulate information, taking the information from sensory systems and storing it in long-term memory (Baddley, 1986). The phonological loop processes auditory information. The visuospatial sketchpad processes visual information. Dual-coding theory describes the two separate systems as aiding each other in representing and processing information (Pavio, 1986). The two subsystems of the working memory can function as independent elements from one another, but learning performance increases as the two systems work in conjunction (Sweller, van Merrienboer, & Pass, 1998). Learning ability increases as information is presented both verbally and visually.

Research has found that verbal and visual representations of information have shown strengths when presented individually. Some studies have found support for visual presentations producing greater recall than verbal presentations (Burton, 1982; Burton & Bruning, 1982). Other studies have shown evidence that verbal presentations are better in gaining the attention of individuals than visual presentations (Bishop & Cates, 2001). The combination of these visual and verbal elements demonstrates improved performance in both areas as opposed to the individual use of these elements.

Application of Cognitive Theories

The concepts and theories of learning and memory provide a theoretical background that allows research to examine classroom learning. Research shows support for improvements in learning when using notes and participation activities. The improvements in learning that result from note taking and participation can be explained by the cognitive theories and processes that have been reviewed. Understanding the roles that the cognitive processes have in such classroom activities as note taking and participation activities helps to maximize the effects of such approaches to instruction and learning.

Cognitive theories applied to participation.

Petress (2006) defined classroom participation as "students being actively engaged, supportive of each other, and civil in their exchanges" (p. 821). De Róiste, Kelly, Molcho, Gavin, and Gabhainn (2012) found that class participation contributed to improved learning performance among children. As students participate in classes, they process the information at a deeper level than if they were to passively attend class. Konings, Brand-Gruwel, and van Merrienboer (2010) demonstrated a participatory model of instruction in high schools. In their model, the students and teachers asked questions of one another and adjusted the class curriculum as the discussion proceeded to create more interaction between students and teachers. The study used a depth of processing approach to support higher levels of learning in participation-based environments. The students and teachers reported higher levels of engagement in the model, but the evaluation scores were not found to be significantly different than students following routine instructional methods. Support for participation has been found in online courses through discussion boards and virtual interaction between peers (Licona & Gurung, 2011; Schuck, 2003; Cheng, Pare, Collimore, & Joorden, 2011). The research found that encouraging participation was beneficial even if the instructor did not participate. The interactions between learners encouraged a deeper processing of the material and a better understanding of the material.

Classroom participation involves the elaboration of concepts through discussion. The discussion allows for the targeted items for learning to be expanded on and connected to other concepts known by the individual. Willoughby, Wood, McDermott, and McLaren (2000) found that discussion-based groups that allowed for elaboration of information performed better on memory tasks than individual self-study groups. The research showed that elaboration of information improved the individuals' memories for the material better than simple studying of the material alone. Along with elaboration, discussion breaks down the information and connects the components of the new information to existing schemata. Schemata allow quicker and easier cognitive access to the concepts and information, but schematic connections present the possibility of false recall.Koriat, Goldsmith, and Pansky (2000) attributed an increase in false memories to the use of schemata in memory formations. False memories could be created by individuals in groups adopting incorrect concepts about the information as presented by group members. Concerns over memory accuracy can be mitigated during class discussions and participation activities by instructor direction and guidance on learning the new information.

Classroom participation uses the depth of processing approach to learning and the self-referencing effect. As students engage in discussion amongst one another, opinions are formed and developed concerning the topic of discussion. Slade and Onion (1995) demonstrated improved recall and retention of information among individuals who had learned medical terms through deep levels of processing as opposed to individuals who had learned terms through shallow means. The research showed that questions referring to the semantic or deeper meaning of the term created a better memory for the term than shallow questions that referred to the structure of the word. In classroom discussions, the participants would be developing connections between memory traces based on the semantic meanings of concepts through discussions. In a non-participating environment, the connections to the concept would be lesser due to fewer semantic associations made between the learned concept and other concepts. In the case of controversial topics, individuals would form opinions based on how the concept relates to themselves. This opinion of the material would allow the individual to reference himself in relation to the learned material. In making a cognitive connection between the learned material and the self, many cognitive connections and associations would form between the new material and the other concepts associated with the individual's concept of self. Howe and Blick (1989) demonstrated an improvement in recall of words when the words were processed through self-reference. The study did not show an effect when the participants were tested for recall of the words after three weeks. The shortcoming of the study was that the researchers used obscure words, which were difficult to connect to other concepts related to the individuals' concepts of themselves. With concepts that are more concrete and relatable to previously known information, the memory trace for the new material can develop connections that are stronger and more stable over time.

Cognitive theories applied to note

taking.

Lecture style classes consist of instructors presenting information to classes that listen to the material, but the students do not participate in open discussion. In the lecture style class, three cognitive theories contribute to retention of information by the students. The first theory is the encoding specificity principle. During the lecture, the students take notes on the material presented by the instructor. The students, similar to how they would respond on an examination, write these notes on paper. The medium of writing serves as a specific manner of encoding the information that is used again to recall the information later (Thieman, 1984). The act of writing serves as a cue for the recall of the information to be a similar format to how the information was originally received during the original lecture.

The organization of memory traces in long-term memory supports the effectiveness of note taking. Schultz and Di Vesta (1972) demonstrated that individuals who took notes on information while reading passages showed significantly better rates of recall than individuals who did not take notes. The researchers attributed the improvement in recall to the clustering of information in an orderly and logical manner through the use of taking notes. Rosenhan, Eisner, and Robinson (1994) found note taking to attribute to the accuracy of recall by jurors in trials. In the study, the organization of notes significantly correlated with the accuracy of recall by the jurors. Mathews (1938) found that high school students showed significant improvement on recall of information when taking notes as opposed to not taking notes. The study demonstrated significant differences between the groups during immediate recall and after a one-month delay. Mathews (1938) showed that the students who took notes recalled the information in a manner that was organized similar to how they wrote the information in their notes. The studies demonstrated support for note taking over passively attending to the information in improving memory for the information but do not give a comparison to participants interacting with the information. Wittrock

(1974) described note taking as a generative process. In a generative process, the student uses the notes actively during the lecture to make connections between the information presented by the lecturer and prior experiences. The process of note taking is an active process due to the mental manipulation of information by the student while organizing the information into a notational format.

The dual coding theory is the third cognitive theory to support the idea that note taking improves memory. In the lecture setting, the verbal presentation of the information by the lecturer serves as one medium of encoding the information. The act of writing the information on paper serves as a second medium of encoding the information. Through the two mediums, the working memory is encoding the learned information into long-term memory through multiple media (Mayer & Sims, 1994). A student processes the information as auditory by hearing the lecturer and visually as the student sees the notes. As the student organizes the notes, mental images representing the organization and structure of the notes are encoded in long-term memory. By processing the information through two mediums, the recall of the information is improved (Clark & Paivio, 1991). The dual coding research has focused on encoding the information visually through use of pictures and has found significant improvements in memory when information was presented verbally and visually using images (Mayer & Sims, 1994). Note taking would also include a mechanical element of encoding as the individual would encode the information through process of physically writing the information.

Conflicting Research

Support against participation.

The use of classroom participation has been shown to facilitate interactions between students to increase knowledge by a flow of information between the students. In situations that involve mass participation, a small number of students have shown high levels of participation while others have decreased in levels of participation (North, Linley, & Hargreaves, 2000). The concept of social loafing occurs when several individuals do not contribute to a task or discussion while others participate at higher levels. The non-participating members of the group are not noticed due to the excess participatory levels of others who compensate for their lack of participation (Ferrari & Pychyl, 2012). When examining the effect of classroom participation across a group of students, social loafing will affect the net benefits of participatory activities. The individuals who failed to interact during discussions and group activities would demonstrate lower than usual levels of learning. The non-benefiting individual's lower scores would lower the rates of learning by acting as outliers. As a result, the effects of participation-based learning would be less significant when examining the results of the class as a whole.

Paulus (2009) examined discussion boards used in online classes. She found that the discussion topics of the students frequently differed from the subject being taught. The discussions boards were to be used as a medium to discuss the concepts being taught in the class; however, the discussions made connections to irrelevant information and resulted in the discussions containing conversations that did not promote learning related to the course's subject matter. Brainerd and Kingma (1986) demonstrated that the organization of how memories are stored in long term memory result in better recall than the number of connections between memories traces in long term memory. The connections in the discussions and classroom participation have been shown to have multiple connections to various concepts in long-term memory.

These connections are often to topics that are unrelated to other information presented in the class. The cognitive connections would result in learning objectives being unconnected to one another and confusion due to the levels of mental disorganization created during the participatory activities.

Support against note taking.

Wittrock (1973) explained that numerous cognitive processes occur during note taking across several verbal, visual, and mechanical processes. When considering the number of processes occurring simultaneously, a cognitive overload could occur with the learner. The cognitive load is represented by the amount of mental effort the individual exerts when performing a particular task (Cooper, 1990). The cognitive load consists of the amount of information processed by an individual through a particular medium (Sweller, van Merrienboer, & Pass, 1998). If an individual attempts to process too much information through a particular medium at one time, the working memory will not be able to accommodate the information and the effectiveness of learning decreases (McCrudden, Schraw, & Hartley, 2004). The limit to the amount of information that can be cognitively processed by an individual poses a problem for Wittrock's (1970) explanation of how note taking improves memory due to the high level of mental processing that occurs during note taking activities.

Research has challenged the idea that notes serve to organize memory traces into logical connections and patterns. Carter and Van Matre (1975) found the act of note taking to serve a minimal role in encoding functions. The researchers found that the notes served as a means of storing information in an external manner. Improved recall of information was found to only be significant if the individual reviewed the notes at a later time. They found the practicing of recall to be effective in memory improvement as opposed to the act of note taking. Similar studies have supported the findings of Carter and Van Matre (1975) by examining the recall of individuals immediately and at later intervals for recall of the material (Fisher & Harris, 1973; Hartley & Davies, 1978; Kobayashi, 2006). Research has shown that the effects of memory improvement from note taking can be attributed to the review of the material instead of the act of annotating the information into a written form.

The Current Study

Past research on note taking and participation in class has focused on one of the learning methods as compared to passive state of learning. Research has demonstrated that both methods of learning are active processes (Wittrock, 1974; Petress, 2006). The current research has failed to effectively compare the processes to one another directly. In comparing the two processes, one may be able to determine several important elements associated with learning processes. By directly comparing the two processes, the effectiveness of each process could be compared to determine the degree to which each process accounts for learning. By understanding the differences, curricula could be designed to take full advantage of the processes of both note taking and participatory learning to improve the encoding and retrieval of learned information from long-term memory. Restructuring of the educational system would improve learning and maximize the amount of information being presented, learned, and replicated by students.

The current study will examine the differences in recall of learned information between students in traditional lectures-style classes and participation-based classes. The findings will examine how students differ on the recall of information on measures that have simple questions, difficult questions, and applied questions. Research supports improved recall of simple information among note taking groups due to the encoding specificity effect and the organization of memory traces (Moscovitch & Craik, 1976; Nairne, 2005; Matthews, 1938). Research supports improved recall of difficult and applied questions among participation groups due to the depth of processing and self-reference effects (Craik & Lockhart, 1972; Willoughby et al., 2000; Slade & Onion, 1995). In comparing the two classroom techniques across different types of examination questions, research can demonstrate the relationship between the teaching-style and effectiveness in recalling information. The researchers expect to find that the note taking groups will show improved recall on simple questions, and the participation groups will show improved recall on difficult and applied questions.

Method

Participants

A convenience sample of 120 undergraduate students from Marshall University will be used. Participants will be students in one of four Introductory Psychology classes. Each class will consist of thirty students. Participants will be informed that participation in the study will fulfill course requirements.

Materials

A common PowerPoint presentation of 25 slides will be used by all classes to serve as an outline of covered material. A stopwatch will be used for time-keeping purposes. The presentation will be displayed on a projection screen at the front of the class with all groups during the instructional period.

One of three versions of a test will be given to the participants during the testing period. The tests consist of multiple-choice questions and utilize scantron sheets for marking answers to the questions. The first question of each test will tell the student to fill in A, B, or C on the Scantron answer sheet depending on the version of the test. Each of the remaining nine questions on the test focused on one of nine target concepts that will be covered in the PowerPoint. Each version will ask one question regarding each of the nine concepts. Each version would have three easy questions, three hard questions, and three applied questions. The easy and hard questions will be chosen from the exams administered during prior semesters.

The difficulty-levels of the questions will be determined based on item-characteristic curves from the 376 students who were administered the questions in the prior year. The questions that are answered correctly by more than 95% of the students that were administered the exam will be defined as easy questions. The questions that were answered correctly less than 80% of the time will be selected as hard questions. Applied questions will be created by faculty to have a medium level of difficulty, as predicted by faculty with expertise in the related target concept areas.

Procedure

On the first day, all participants will be presented with informed consent forms at the beginning of class. One morning and one afternoon class will receive the lecture model of instruction. During the same time frames, one other morning class and one other afternoon class will receive instruction by the participation-based model. In the lecture classes, the participants will be instructed to take notes on the lecture presented to them and to refrain from asking questions or interacting with the lecturer. The participants will receive one hour and fifteen minutes of instruction covering general concepts of social psychology. Prior to class, the instructor will be briefed that he should follow the outline that of the PowerPoint and refrain from wandering off topic. Adequate time will be given for the instructors to familiarize themselves with the outline. Upon completion of the class, the participants will be permitted to take their notes with them and review them.

For the participation-based classes, the participants will be informed that were not to take any notes and will be instructed to put away all note-taking materials at the beginning of the class session. They will be told to ask at least 3 questions or provide 3 statements per student during the class, instead of using notes. The instructor will use the same PowerPoint presentation as the lecture-based classes. To encourage participation through discussion, the instructor will ask random participants to read a bullet from the outline and provide feedback throughout the class. The participation-based classes will be given one hour and fifteen minutes to discuss the material.

Two days after the instruction class, participants will be evaluated on how they could recall information from the prior class. At the beginning of the second day of class, participants will be given the ten-question, multiple-choice tests to evaluate their understanding of the nine target concepts. In each class, ten participants will be given version A; ten participants will be given version B; and ten participants will be given version C. Prior to passing out the tests, participants will be instructed to put away all notes and books and not to begin the test until told to do so. The versions will be shuffled and provided to the participants in random assignment of the test versions.

The questions will be passed out to the participants turned face down with a unique number on the back of each test that ranges from one to thirty. The participants will be instructed not to write on the question sheets. After the participants received the question sheets, the Scantron forms will be passed out to the participants. The participants will be instructed not to fill out their names on the Scantron forms. The participants will be instructed to bubble in their course section number in the special information box followed by the unique identifying number on the back of their question sheet. Once all participants fill in the corresponding bubbles in the special information section of the Scantron forms, the participants will be told that the first question would tell them to fill in a specific bubble for question one. The instructor will inform the participants that they would have fifteen minutes to complete all questions and to turn their Scantron form in face down on a desk at the front of the room. They will also told to fill in the first question as indicated by the statement for question one. The participants will then be told to turn over their tests and begin. At the end of the fifteen minutes, the instructor will announce that the time is up for any remaining participants to answer questions, and the participants will be instructed to pass any remaining test to the front of the room to be collected.

Statistics

The results will be analyzed using an ANOVA to determine if there is a significant difference between the lecture-based and participation-based methods of instruction across easy, hard, and applied questions. The critical value will be set at .05. The results will then be compared across types of questions using a Student–Newman–Keuls post-hoc analysis to determine pairwise comparisons across the groups.

References

Anderson, R. C., Reynolds, R. E., Schallert, D. L., & Goetz,
E. T. (1977). Frameworks for comprehending
discourse. *American Educational Research Journal,
14*(4), 367-381.

Atkinson, R. C., & Shiffrin, R.M. (1968). Human memory: A
proposed system and its

control process. In K.W. Spence & J. T. Spence
(Eds.), *The psychology of*

*learning and motivation: Advances in research and
theory* (Vol. 2, pp.353-380).

New York: Academic Press.

Baddeley, A. (1986). Working Memory. New York, NY.
Oxford University Press.

Bishop, M. J., & Cates, W. M. (2001). Theoretical
foundations for sound's use in

multimedia instruction to enhance learning. *Journal
of Education, Training,*

Research and Development, *49*(3), 5-22.

Burton, J. K. (1982). Dual coding of pictorial stimuli. *Journal of Mental Imagery, 6*, 159-

168.

Burton, J. K., & Bruning, R. H. (1982). Interference effects on the recall of pictures,

printed words and spoken words. *Contemporary Educational Psychology, 7*, 61-

69.

Brainerd, C. J., Kingma, J., & Howe, M. L. (1986). Spread of encoding and the development of organization in memory. *Canadian Journal of Psychology/Revue Canadienne de Psychologie, 40*(3), 203.

Carter, J. F., & Van Matre, N. H. (1975). Note taking versus note having. *Journal of Educational Psychology, 67*(6), 900.

Cheng, C., Pare, D. E., Collimore, L., & Joordens, S. (2011). Assessing the Effectiveness of a Voluntary Online Discussion Forum on Improving Students' Course Performance. *Computers & Education, 56*(1), 253-261.

Clark, J. M., & Paivio, A. (1991). Dual coding theory and

education. *Educational Psychology Review, 3*(3), 149-210. doi:10.1007/BF01320076

Cooper, G. (1990). Cognitive load theory as an aid for instructional design. *Australian Journal of Educational Technology, 6*(2), 108-113.

Craik, F. I., & Lockhart, R. S. (1972). Levels of processing: A framework for memory research. *Journal of Verbal Learning & Verbal Behavior, 11*(6), 671-684. doi:10.1016/S0022-5371(72)80001-X

de Róiste, A., Kelly, C., Molcho, M., Gavin, A., & Gabhainn, S. (2012). Is school participation good for children? Associations with health and wellbeing. *Health Education, 112*(2), 88-104. doi:10.1108/09654281211203394

Ferrari, J. R., & Pychyl, T. A. (2012). 'If I wait, my partner will do it': The role of conscientiousness as a mediator in the relation of academic procrastination and perceived social loafing. *North American Journal of Psychology, 14*(1), 13-24.

Fisher, J. L., & Harris, M. B. (1973). Effect of note taking and review on recall. *Journal of Educational Psychology, 65*(3), 321.

Hardman, F., Smith, F., & Wall, K. (2003). 'Interactive Whole

Class Teaching' in the National Literacy
Strategy. *Cambridge Journal of Education, 33*(2),
197-215. doi:10.1080/03057640302043

Hartley, J., & Davies, I. K. (1978). Note-taking: A critical
review. *Programmed Learning and Educational
Technology*, *15*(3), 207-224

Howe, J. B., & Blick, K. A. (1989). Retention of word
meanings as a function of depth of
processing. *Perceptual and Motor Skills, 69*(1), 195-
198. doi:10.2466/pms.1989.69.1.195

Kobayashi, K. (2006). Combined Effects of
Note-Taking/-Reviewing on Learning and the
Enhancement through Interventions: A meta-analytic
review. *Educational Psychology*, *26*(3), 459-477.

Konings, K. D., Brand-Gruwel, S., & van Merrienboer, J. G.
(2010). An Approach to Participatory Instructional
Design in Secondary Education: An Exploratory
Study. *Educational Research, 52*(1), 45-59.

Koriat, A., Goldsmith, M., & Pansky, A. (2000). Toward a
psychology of memory accuracy. *Annual Review of
Psychology, 51*, 481-537.
doi:10.1146/annurev.psych.51.1.481

Licona, M. M., & Gurung, B. (2011). Asynchronous

Discussions in Online Multicultural
Education. *Multicultural Education, 19*(1), 2-8.

Marcuse, F. L. (1951). On methods of teaching elementary
psychology. *Journal of Educational Psychology,
42*(4), 236-240. doi:10.1037/h0059656

Mathews, C. O. (1938). Comparison of methods of study for
immediate and delayed recall. *Journal of
Educational Psychology, 29*(2), 101-106.
doi:10.1037/h0055182

McCrudden, M., Schraw, G., Hartley, K., & Kenneth, A. K.
(2004). The influence of presentation, organization,
and example context on text learning. *The Journal of
experimental education, 72*(4), 289-306.

McNamara, T. P., & Holbrook, J. B. (2003). Semantic
memory and priming. In I. B. Weiner
(Eds.), *Handbook of psychology* (445-474).
Hoboken, NJ: John Wiley and Sons, Inc.

Mayer, R. E., & Sims, V. K. (1994). For whom is a picture
worth a thousand words? Extensions of a dual-
coding theory of multimedia learning. *Journal of
Educational Psychology, 86*(3), 389-401.
doi:10.1037/0022-0663.86.3.389

Moscovitch, M., & Craik, F. I. (1976). Depth of processing,

retrieval cues, and uniqueness of encoding as factors in recall. *Journal of Verbal Learning and Verbal Behavior, 15*(4), 447-458.

Nairne, J. S. (2005). The functionalist agenda in memory. In A. F. Healy (Ed.), *Experimental Cognitive Psychology and Its Applications* (pp. 115-126). Washington, DC: American Psychological Association. doi: 10.1037/10895-009

North, A. C., Linley, P. A., & Hargreaves, D. J. (2000). Social loafing in a co-operative classroom task. *Educational Psychology, 20*(4), 389-392.

Paivio, A. (1986). *Mental representations: A dual-coding approach.* New York, New

York: Oxford University Press.

Paulus, T. M. (2009). Online but Off-Topic: Negotiating Common Ground in Small Learning Groups. Instructional Science: *An International Journal of the Learning Sciences, 37*(3), 227-245.

Peterson, L., & Peterson, M. J. (1959). Short-term retention of individual verbal items. *Journal of Experimental Psychology, 58*(3), 193.

Petress, K. (2006). An Operational Definition of Class Participation. *College Student Journal, 40*(4), 821-

823.

Rogers, T. B., Kuiper, N. A., & Kirker, W. S. (1977). Self-reference and the encoding of personal information. *Journal of Personality and Social Psychology, 35*(9), 677-688.

Rosenhan, D. L., Eisner, S. L., & Robinson, R. J. (1994). Note taking can aid juror recall. *Law And Human Behavior, 18*(1), 53-61. doi:10.1007/BF01499143

Schultz, C. B., & Di Vesta, F. J. (1972). Effects of passage organization and note taking on the selection of clustering strategies and on recall of textual materials. *Journal of Educational Psychology, 63*(3), 244-252. doi:10.1037/h0032651

Schuck, S. (2003). The Use of Electronic Question and Answer Forums in Mathematics Teacher Education. *Mathematics Teacher Education And Development, 5*, 19-31.

Slade, P. D., & Onion, C. R. (1995). Depth of Information Processing and Memory for Medical Facts. *Medical Teacher, 17*(3), 307-13.

Smith, E. E., Shoben, E. J., & Rips, L. J. (1974). Structure and process in semantic memory: A featural model for semantic decisions. *Psychological Review, 81*(3),

214.

Sweller, J., van Merrienboer, J. G., & Pass, F. G. W. (1998). Cognitive architecture and

instructional design. *Educational Psychology Review, 10*(3), 251-296.

Thieman, T. J. (1984). A Classroom Demonstration of Encoding Specificity. *Teaching of Psychology, 11*(2), 101-02

Tulving, E. (1993). What is episodic memory? *Current Directions in Psychological*

Science, 2, 67-70.

Tulving, E., & Madigan, S. A. (1970). Memory and verbal learning. *Annual Review of Psychology, 21*(1), 437-484.

U.S. Department of Education. (2008). *Great Expectations: Holding Ourselves and Our Schools Accountable for Results*, Washington, DC: Government Printing Office.

Wittrock, M. C. (1974). Learning as a generative process. *Educational Psychologist, 11,* 87– 95.

Willoughby, T., Wood, E., McDermott, C., & McLaren, J. (2000). Enhancing learning through strategy

instruction and group interaction: Is active
generation of elaborations critical?. *Applied
Cognitive Psychology, 14*(1), 19-30.
doi:10.1002/(SICI)1099-
0720(200001)14:1<19::AID-ACP619>3.0.CO;2-4

Woodall, W. G., & Folger, J. P. (1981). Encoding specificity
and nonverbal cue context: An expansion of episodic
memory research. *Communications
Monographs, 48*(1), 39-53.
doi:10.1080/03637758109376046

www.ingramcontent.com/pod-product-compliance
Lightning Source LLC
Chambersburg PA
CBHW020902310526
45786CB00018B/1596